The Dachshund

Elizabeth Harrap

GW00383094

John Bartholomew & Son Limited
Edinburgh and London

The Publisher wishes to thank The Kennel Club and The American Kennel Club for permission to reproduce the breed standards.

First published in Great Britain 1977 *by*
JOHN BARTHOLOMEW & SON LIMITED
12 Duncan Street, Edinburgh EH9 1TA
And at 216 High Street, Bromley BR1 1PW

ISBN 0 7028 1025 8

1st edition

Prepared for the Publisher by Youé & Spooner Ltd.
Colour illustrations by Charles Rush; airbrush drawings by Malcolm Ward

Printed in Great Britain by John Bartholomew & Son Limited

Contents

A beautiful Long-haired Dachshund

Preface

Here is a book devoted to one of the best known and widely kept of companion dogs, that loving humourist on short legs, the Dachshund. This is a breed which every layman recognises. Though they have been the butt of many jokes and burdened with ridiculous nicknames, all who own Dachshunds are united in their admiration for a sporting dog of great charm and character. The author who has owned the breed for many years describes all six varieties in detail. All aspects of Dachshund care are fully covered from choosing your first puppy to showing your first dog. New owners will find all they need to know and those who have already fallen for the charms of this breed will still gain much by reading this book.

Wendy Boorer
Consultant Editor

Breed history

The Dachshund or Teckel, so often caricatured because of its shape, is a breed of great versatility. It is courageous, loyal and full of character. It can go to ground after vermin, hunt and retrieve game, walk for miles enjoying every minute or entertain the family with its many winning ways. Once you have owned a Dachshund, or rather a Dachshund has owned you, you will be a slave of the breed for ever.

The origin of the Dachshund is somewhat doubtful, some sources tracing a similar type of dog to ancient Egypt. Long-bodied, short-legged hunting dogs with hound-like ears have certainly been known on the continent since medieval times. It is impossible now to tell whether these were Basset Hounds or Dachshunds, or whether indeed both these breeds sprang from this same root. However, even then, these dogs were distinguished by their tracking ability, and their courage and capacity for working underground against vermin, and for badger hunting.

The Dachshund derives its name from its early use in badger hunting. The dog was required to dig and drive the badgers from their sets to the waiting guns of the huntsmen. A badger makes a formidable opponent when brought to bay and the Dachshund had to show great courage to tackle such a foe. They were also used, and still are in Germany, to go after foxes, being expected to enter the earths and draw the fox to the surface where the hounds or guns would be waiting.

The construction of the Dachshund, with its long body and oval rib cage to allow plenty of room for heart and lungs, enables it to work underground with the maximum efficiency.

These hunting instincts are inherent in the breed today and were always of paramount importance to the German breeders who developed the breed.

The earliest of German all breed stud books, published in 1840, records fifty-four Dachshunds and it is probable that even then the smooth and the long-haired varieties were firmly established as separate types. As well as drawing foxes and badgers, Dachshunds in Germany are expected to be able to range and flush areas of undergrowth, and to track game wounded or otherwise. The quarry might vary in size from a roe deer to a rabbit, and the dogs are expected to bay when they are on the scent.

Early Long-haired varieties were used for hunting

Points of the Dachshund

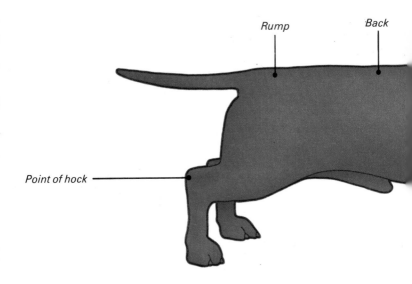

Rump

Back

Point of hock

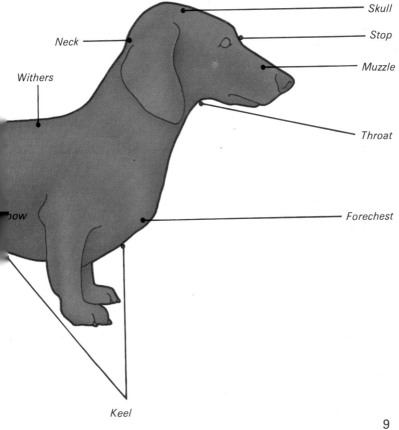

Skull

Stop

Neck

Muzzle

Withers

Throat

bow

Forechest

Keel

9

In America the importation of the smooth Dachshund antedates the first organised dog shows or stud books. In Britain, Prince Albert, consort to Queen Victoria, introduced the breed from Germany in the 1840s. He used them when he went shooting, and royal patronage quickly made them popular. Throughout the years the British royal family have been admirers of the breed with the present Queen Mother owning miniature smooths. In 1881 the Dachshund Club was formed, becoming one of the first breed clubs in the country.

In both countries, the Dachshund suffered a disastrous decline in the First World War owing to public prejudice against anything German. There are sad records of Dachshunds and their owners being stoned in London streets. From being among the ten most popular breeds in America, registrations fell rapidly until immediately postwar there were a mere dozen or so, necessitating further importations to replenish the breeding stock. However, the breed's second rise to popularity was not checked so dramatically by the outbreak of World War II and on both sides of the Atlantic they remain firm public favourites.

The Long-haired Dachshund made its first appearance in Britain in 1920 and because of its glamorous coat soon became popular. The Wire-haired has never attained much popularity and remains the least known of the three varieties. The Miniature Dachshund was first produced in Germany by sportsmen who wanted a smaller dog to go after rabbits. A certain amount of cross-breeding took place which reduced the size but produced a rather variegated type. British breeders bred down from small standard Dachshunds which led to size problems but kept type more constant. When considering the Dachshund as a pet, one should always remember the breed's sporting background and abilities. There is nothing sadder than seeing a gross, obese Dachshund waddling along city pavements, and comparing it to the alert, courageous, muscular hunting dog that it should be. However, the breed's distinctive shape and the ease with which it can be caricatured, have tended to obscure in the public's mind its true hound nature. Elaborate field trials run by the Deutscher Teckelclub in Germany still test the breed's hunting capabilities. The American Kennel Club also has trials which test the dog's tracking abilities, but these activities are very much a minority interest and the majority of Dachshunds live simply as pets.

Early Smooth-haired Dachshunds

The characters of the six varieties are best summarised by quoting the descriptions given under the heading 'Characteristics' in the British Kennel Club standards for the breeds.

'First and foremost a sporting dog, the Smooth Dachshund is remarkably versatile, being equally adaptable as a house pet; his smooth, close coat is impervious to rain and mud. His temperament and acute intelligence make him the ideal companion for town or country. In the field of sport he is unequalled, combining the scenting powers of a Foxhound with unflinching courage, and will go to ground to fox, otter or badger.'

'The Long-haired Dachshund is an old, fixed sub-variety of the "Teckel", and its history extends back to the beginning of Teckel breeding. The breed is full of character, quick in attack and defence, faithful when properly brought up and very obedient. All the senses are well developed. It has the reputation of being extraordinarily intelligent and easy to train. Its build and temperament fit it to hunt quarry both above and below ground; its eagerness, keen sight and hearing and its sonorous bark make it especially suitable for tracking. In these respects it compares very favourably with any other variety. The thick, soft hair protects it against thorns, enables it to endure both cold and heat and is rain-proof. It is especially suited to water work. In following a trail its highly developed sense of smell stands it in good stead. It is easily trained to retrieve. The Long-haired Dachshund can therefore be used in many different ways by the sportsman.'

'The Wire-haired Dachshund should be clever, lively, courageous to the point of rashness, sagacious and obedient. He is especially suited for going to ground because of his low build, very strong forequarters and forelegs, long, strong jaw and the immense power of his bite and hold. His loose skin enables him to manoeuvre with ease for attack or defence. His deep, loud bay indicates his position to those working him. He is also well equipped for field work on account of his good nose and sound construction. He can force his way through cover so dense that it would stop even the smallest gundog. Because of his nose, voice, good sight and perseverance he makes a good tracking dog.'

'The Miniature Dachshund should be gay, alert, bold and highly intelligent. Despite its small size it should be strong, extremely active, hardy and game. Movement should be free and gay. Both fore and hind feet should move straight forward without plaiting or crossing in front and free from any tendency to throw out the hind feet sideways.'

These characteristics are not only what we should expect from each variety but also what we should endeavour to preserve in this fascinating breed. The physical requirements for each of the three coats are basically the same but the finer points of temperament are different. The Smooth-haired Dachshund is very much a one person dog. While it will give love and affection to all the family, there will always be one member to whom it gives its special allegiance. It is not particularly interested in getting to know strangers and is often aloof. The Smooth likes its home comforts, especially after a day's hunting.

The Long-haired Dachshund is the glamorous variety of the breed and with its shining, silky coat and proud head carriage has gained a large following over the years. It is not such a one man dog as the Smooth, being equally happy and playful with all members of the family. The standard Long-hair of today is much larger than in the past. It is a strong dog and does need firm handling on occasions.

The Wire-haired Dachshund, the least known of the three coats, is the complete extrovert. It loves all and sundry and with its amusing ways is winning over an ever-increasing following. As with the standard Long, the standard Wire has become much larger over the years. The male Wire-haired Dachshund, while being a first rate companion, is a tough dog which does not always tolerate other males and will fight if given the chance. As the Breed Standard states, the dog has strong jaws and immense power in its bite and hold, and this it can use with great effect. But, providing the dog is brought up correctly and not allowed to get into a position where it could meet another dominant male, either on its home ground or over a bitch, this should not prevent a would-be purchaser from owning one of these delightful dogs. As with all breeds there are those members who will fight among themselves and, while Dachshunds are no worse than others, it is better to know that these jealousies can occur.

The Dachshund is a suitable pet for either town or country, with the Miniature being especially suited to urban living because of its small size. However, the hunting instinct is still very much present. A Dachshund loves to dig, be it in the garden, fields or woods. If you are a very keen gardener you may not appreciate this trait. It also means that any fencing to keep the dog in must be securely buried in the ground so that your Dachshund has no chance of digging its way out, perhaps to indulge in its passion for hunting.

The Dachshund is an excellent house dog, as its deep bark belies its size. Any intruders would receive an unpleasant welcome, for Dachshunds are great ones for nipping ankles. However, there is a point to be watched, for Dachshunds can become incessant barkers. They will bark at people passing the house and at noises of all kinds. In this respect the owner must be firm from the beginning and not allow the habit to develop.

Dachshunds can be obstinate, doing only what they want to do when they want to do it! They also have, on occasions, the annoying habit of 'going deaf'. This usually occurs at the end of a walk when you want to put them on the lead and they would rather continue going about their own business! The look on the face of a Dachshund when it pretends it cannot hear you is highly amusing. It will turn to look you full in the face, as if to say, 'Did you call?' and then turn back to the business on hand, oblivious to anything but its own interests!

The Dachshund is a highly intelligent dog and knows when it has done wrong. The guilty look on the face when a misdemeanour has been discovered always gives the game away. But then, who can scold a dog which proceeds to roll over on its back waving its feet helplessly in the air?

If you want a dog that is full of character and fun, and sporting with it, then the Dachshund cannot be bettered. It is excellent with children providing the children are sensible (no dog should ever be teased), and will give many years of immense pleasure. The charm and success of the Dachshund as a pet are best summarised by George Meredith's epitaph to his own dog: 'There lived with us a wagging humorist, in that hound's arch dwarf-legged on boxing gloves.'

A standard Smooth-haired

The breed standards

The British Standards

Long-haired

Characteristics *The Long-haired Dachshund is an old, fixed sub-variety of the "Teckel", and its history extends back to the beginning of Teckel breeding. The breed is full of character, quick in attack and defence, faithful when properly brought up and very obedient. All the senses are well developed. It has the reputation of being extraordinarily intelligent and easy to train. Its build and temperament fit it to hunt quarry both above and below ground; its eagerness, keen sight and hearing and its sonorous bark make it especially suitable for tracking. In these respects it compares very favourably with any other variety. The thick, soft hair protects it against thorns, enables it to endure both cold and heat and is rain-proof. It is especially suited to water work. In following a trail its highly developed sense of smell stands it in good stead. It is easily trained to retrieve. The Long-haired Dachshund can therefore be used in many different ways by the sportsman.*

General Appearance *Form, colour, size and character similar in all respects to those of the Smooth Dachshund, except for the long, soft hair. The form is compact, short-legged and long, but sinewy and well muscled, with bold and defiant head carriage, and intelligent expression. In spite of the shortness of the legs the body should be neither too plump nor so slender as to have a weasel-like appearance. Height at shoulder should be half the length of the body measured from the breast bone to the set-on of the tail, and the girth of the chest double the height at the shoulder. The length from the tip of the nose to the eyes should be equal to the length from the eyes to the base of the skull. The tail should not touch the ground when at rest, neither should the ears (i.e. the leather) extend beyond the nose when pulled to the front.*

Head and Skull *Long and conical when seen from above, and in profile, sharp and finely modelled. Skull neither too broad nor too narrow, only slightly arched, without prominent stop. Foreface long and finely modelled. Lips should be tightly drawn, well covering the lower jaw, neither too heavy nor too sharply cut away, the corners of the mouth slightly marked.*

Eyes *Medium in size, oval, set obliquely, clear, expressive and dark in colour.*

Ears *Broad and placed relatively well back, high and well set on lying close to the cheeks, broad and long, nicely feathered and very mobile.*

Mouth *Wide, extending back to behind the eyes, furnished with strong teeth which should fit into one another exactly, the inner side of the upper incisors closing on the outer side of the under ones.*

Neck *Sufficiently long, muscular, showing no dewlap, slightly arched at the nape, running gracefully into the shoulders, carried well up and forward.*

Forequarters *Muscular, with deep chest. Shoulders long and broad, set obliquely, lying firmly on well developed ribs. Muscles hard and plastic. Breast bone prominent, extending so far forward as to show depressions on both sides. Upper arm the same length as the shoulder blade, jointed at right angles to the shoulder, well boned and muscled, set on close to the ribs but moving freely as far as the shoulder blade. Lower arm comparatively short, inclined slightly inwards, solid and well muscled.*

Body *Long and well muscled, the back showing oblique shoulders and short and strong pelvic region. Ribs very oval, deep between the forelegs and extending far back. Loin short, strong and broad. The line of the back only slightly depressed over the shoulders and slightly arched over the loin, with the outline of the belly moderately tucked up.*

Hindquarters *Rump round, full, broad, with muscles well modelled and plastic. Pelvic bone not too short, broad, strongly developed and set obliquely. Thigh bone strong, of good length and jointed to the pelvis at right angles. Second thigh short, set at right angles to the upper thigh, well muscled. Hocks set wide apart, strongly bent and, seen from behind, the legs should be straight.*

Feet *Broad and large, straight or turned slightly outwards; the hind feet smaller and narrower than the fore. Toes close together and with a distinct arch to each toe. Nails strong. The dog must stand equally on all parts of the foot.*

Tail *Set on fairly high, not too long, tapering and without too marked a curve. Not carried too high. Fully feathered.*

Coat *Soft and straight or slightly waved, of shining colour. Longer under the neck, the underparts of the body and, particularly, on the ears, behind the legs, where it should develop into abundant feathering, and reach the greatest* length on the tail, where it should form a flag. The feathering should extend to the outsides of the ears, where short hair is not desired. Too heavy a coat gives an appearance of undue plumpness and hides the outline. The coat should resemble that of an Irish Setter, giving the dog an appearance of elegance. Too much hair on the feet is ugly and useless.

Colour *Black and tan, dark brown with lighter shadings, dark red, light red, dappled, tiger-marked or brindle. In black and tan, red and dappled dogs the nose and nails should be black, in chocolate they are often brown.*

Weight and Size *As a rule Long-haired Dachshunds are classifed as follows: Middle weight up to 17lb. (7.71kg.) for bitches and 18lb. (8.16kg.) for dogs. Heavy weight over 17lb. (7.71kg.) for bitches and over 18lb. (8.16kg.) for dogs. The Middle-weights are best suited for badger and fox drawing and the Heavy-weights for tracking, hunting larger animals and for water work. The last named are also very useful for retrieving rabbits and water fowl.*

Note *Male animals should have two apparently normal testicles fully descended into the scrotum.*

Smooth-haired

Characteristics *First and foremost a sporting dog, the Smooth Dachshund is remarkably versatile, being equally adaptable as a house pet; his smooth, close coat is impervious to rain and mud. His temperament and acute intelligence make him the ideal companion for town or country. In the field of sport he is unequalled, combining the scenting powers of a Foxhound with unflinching courage, and will go to ground to fox, otter or badger.*

General Appearance *Long and low, but with compact and well-muscled body, not crippled, cloddy, or clumsy, with bold defiant carriage of head and intelligent expression.*

Head and Skull *Long and appearing conical when seen from above, and from a side view tapering to the point of the muzzle. Stop not pronounced, skull should be slightly arched in profile, appearing neither too broad nor too narrow. Jaw neither too square nor snipy but strong, the lips lightly stretched fairly covering the lower jaw.*

Eyes *Medium in size, oval, and set obliquely. Dark in colour, except in the case of Chocolates, in which they may be lighter; in Dapples one or both wall eyes are permissible.*

Ears *Broad, of moderate length, and well rounded (not narrow,* pointed or folded), relatively well back, high and well set on, lying close to the cheek, very mobile as in all intelligent dogs; when at attention the back of the ear directed forward and outward.

Mouth Teeth must be strongly developed. The powerful canine teeth must fit closely. The correct bite is a scissor bite, any deviation being a fault.

Neck Sufficiently long, muscular, clean, no dewlap, slightly arched in the nape, running in graceful lines into the shoulders, carried well up and forward.

Forequarters Shoulder blades long, broad and set on sloping, lying firmly on fully-developed ribs, muscles hard and plastic. Chest very oval, with ample room for the heart and lungs, deep and with ribs well sprung out towards the loins, breast-bone very prominent. The front legs should, when viewed from one side, cover the lowest point of the breastline. Forelegs very short and in proportion to size strong in bone. Upper arm of equal length with, and at right angles to, the shoulder blade; elbows lying close to ribs, but moving freely up to shoulder blades. Lower arm short as compared with other animals, slightly inclined inwards (crook), seen in profile moderately straight; not bending forward or knuckling over (which indicates unsoundness).

Body Long and muscular, the line of back slightly depressed at shoulders and slightly arched over the loin, which should be short and strong; outline of belly moderately tucked up. What is required is a general levelness of the back, the hindquarters (the rump) not being higher than the shoulders.

Hindquarters Rump round, full, broad; muscles hard and plastic; hip bone or pelvic bone not too short, broad and strongly developed, set moderately sloping, thigh bones strong, of good length, and joined to pelvis at right-angles; lower thighs short in comparison with other animals; hocks well developed and seen from behind the legs should be straight (not cow-hocked). The dog should not appear higher at the quarters than at shoulders.

Feet The front feet should be full, broad and close-knit, and straight or very slightly turned outwards, the hind feet smaller and narrower. The toes must be close together with a decided arch to each toe, with strong regularly placed nails and firm pads. The dog must stand true, i.e. equally on all parts of the foot.

Tail *Set on fairly high, stong and tapering, but not too long and not too curved or carried too high.*

Coat *Short, dense and smooth, but strong. The hair on the underside of the tail coarse in texture; skin loose and supple, but fitting the dog closely all over, without much wrinkle.*

Colour *Any colour other than white (except a white spot on breast). Nose and nails should be black. In red dogs a red nose is permissible but not desirable. In Chocolate and Dapples the nose may be brown or flesh-coloured. In Dapples large spots of colour are undesirable, and the dog should be evenly dappled all over.*

Weight and Size *Dogs should not exceed 25lb. (11.35kg.). Bitches should not exceed 23lb. (10.44kg.).*

Faults *In general appearance weak or deformed, too high or too low to the ground; ears set on too high or too low, eyes too prominent; muzzle too short or pinched, either undershot or overshot; forelegs too crooked; hare or terrier feet, or flat spread toes (flat-footed); out at elbows; body too much dip behind the shoulders; loins weak or too arched; chest too flat or too short; hindquarters weak or cow-hocked, quarters higher than the shoulders.*

Note *Male animals should have two apparently normal testicles fully descended into the scrotum.*

Wire-haired

Characteristics *The Dachshund should be clever, lively, courageous to the point of rashness, sagacious and obedient. He is especially suited for going to ground because of his low build, very strong forequarters and forelegs, long, strong jaw and the immense power of his bite and hold. His loose skin enables him to manoeuvre with ease for attack or defence. His deep, loud bay indicates his position to those working him. He is also well equipped for field work on account of his good nose and sound construction. He can force his way through cover so dense that it would stop even the smallest gundog. Because of his nose, voice, good sight and perseverence he makes a good tracking dog.*

General Appearance *Low to ground, short legged, the body long but compact and well muscled. The head should be carried boldly and the expression be very intelligent. Despite his short legs, compared with the length of his body, he must not be awkward, cramped, crippled or lacking in substance.*

Head and Skull *Looked at from above or from the side, the head should taper uniformly to the tip of the nose and be clean cut. The skull is only slightly arched, being neither too broad nor too narrow and slopes gradually, without marked stop, to a finely formed, slightly arched muzzle, the nasal bones and cartilage (septum) being long and narrow. The ridges of the frontal bones are well developed giving prominence to the nerve bosses over the eyes. Jaw has extremely strong bones, is very long and opens very wide. It should not be too square nor yet snipy. The lips are lightly stretched, the corners just marked and the upper lip covers the lower jaw neatly.*

Eyes *Oval, medium in size, set obliquely, lustrous and expressive. The colour should be dark except in the case of chocolates, when they may be lighter, and of dapples, when one or both wall eyes are allowed.*

Ears *Broad and rounded, the front edge touching the cheek. They are relatively well back and high and are well set on. The length is such that when the ears are pulled forward they reach a point approximately half-way between the eyes and the tip of the nose.*

Mouth *The powerful canine teeth fit closely. The correct bite is a scissor bite, any deviation being a fault.*

Neck *Sufficiently long, muscular, clean cut, not showing any dewlap, slightly arched in the nape, extending in a graceful line into the shoulders and carried erect.*

Forequarters *The shoulder blades are long, broad and placed firmly and obliquely upon a very robust rib cage. The upper arm is the same length as the shoulder blade, set at right angles to it and, like the shoulder blade, is very strong and covered with hard but supple muscles. The upper arm lies close to the ribs but is able to move freely. The forearm is comparatively short, inclined slightly inwards to form the crook, when seen in profile is moderately straight and must not bend forward or knuckle over, a state which indicates unsoundness. A correctly placed front leg covers the lowest point of the breast bone.*

Body *The breast bone is strong and prominent enough to show a dimple at each side. Looked at from the front the thorax should be very oval, allowing ample room for the heart and lungs; seen from the side it should intersect the forearm just above the wrist. The top line, very slightly depressed at the shoulders and slightly arched over the loin, is parallel to the* ground. The whole trunk should be long, well ribbed up and underneath should merge gradually into the line of a moderately tucked up belly. The rump is full, round and wide with strong and pliant muscles.

Hindquarters The pelvis is strong, set obliquely and not too short. The upper thigh, set at right angles to the pelvis, is strong and of good length, the lower thigh is short, set at right angles to the upper thigh and is well muscled. The hocks are well developed. The legs when seen from behind, are set well apart, straight and parallel to one another.

Feet The front feet are full, broad in front, straight or turned just a trifle outwards. The four toes forming the foot are compact, well arched and have tough pads. The fifth toe (dewclaw) is usually left on. The nails are strong and short. The dog must stand true and equally on all parts of the foot. The hind feet are smaller and narrower than the fore feet and placed straight. There should be no dewclaw. In all other respects the hind feet and toes are similar to the fore feet and toes.

Tail Continues line of the spine; is but slightly curved, must not be carried too gaily or reach the ground when at rest.

Coat With the exception of the jaw, eyebrows and ears, the whole body is covered with a completely even, short, harsh coat and an undercoat. There should be a beard on the chin. The eyebrows are bushy. The hair on the ears is almost smooth.

Colour All colours are allowed but a white patch on the chest, though not a fault, is not desirable. Except in the case of Chocolates, when it may be brown or flesh-coloured, the nose should be black.

Weight and Size It is recommended that dogs should weigh from 20 to 22lb. (9.07 to 9.98kg.) and bitches from 18 to 20lb. (8.16 to 9.07kg.).

Faults Primary Faults An overshot or undershot jaw. Out at elbow. Knuckling over. Toes turned inwards. Splayed feet. Cow hocks. A bad coat. Secondary Faults Very light eyes. A narrow chest. Breast bone insufficiently prominent. A dip behind the shoulders. A hollow back. A roach back. Rump higher than withers. Weak loins. Excessively drawn up flanks. Bad angulation of forequarters or hindquarters. Legs too long, too close in front, or behind. Toes turned too much outwards. Bowed hind legs. A sluggish, clumsy or waddling gait. Poor *muscle. Too long a tail.* Minor Faults *Ears too high, too low, sticking out, folded or narrow. Too marked a stop. Head too wide, too narrow or too short. Too pointed or too weak a jaw. Short neck or swan neck. Dewlaps. Goggle eyes. Too short a tail.*

Note *Male animals should have two apparently normal testicles fully descended into the scrotum.*

Miniature Long-haired

Characteristics *The Miniature Dachshund should be gay, alert, bold and highly intelligent. Despite its small size it should be strong, extremely active, hardy and game. Movement should be free and gay. Both fore and hind feet should move straight forward without plaiting or crossing in front and free from any tendency to throw out the hind feet sideways.*

General Appearance *In conformation the Miniature Dachshund should be in all respects similar to the Dachshund of standard size. It should be compact, short-legged and long in body, well muscled and strong, with bold and intelligent expression. The body should be neither so plump as to give an impression of cobbiness, nor so slender as to impart a weasel-like appearance. Height at shoulder should be half the length of the body measured from the breast bone to the base of the tail, and the girth of the chest double the height at the shoulder. The length from the tip of the nose to the eyes should equal the length from eyes to base of skull.*

Head and Skull *Long and conical when seen from above, sharp in profile and finely modelled. Skull neither too broad nor too narrow, only slightly arched and without prominent stop. Foreface long and narrow, finely modelled. The lips should be tightly drawn but well covering the lower jaw, neither heavy nor too sharply cut away. The corners of the mouth slightly marked.*

Eyes *Of medium size, neither prominent nor too deeply set, oval in shape placed obliquely. They should be clear and expressive and dark in colour except in Dapples and Chocolates, in which wall or light eyes are permissible.*

Ears *Broad and placed relatively well back, high and well set on, lying close to the cheeks and very mobile. The leather of the ears when pulled to the front should not extend beyond the tip of the nose.*

Mouth *Wide, extending back to behind the eyes. Teeth sound*

and strong, the inner side of the upper incisors closing on the outer side of the under ones.

Neck *Long and muscular, showing no dewlap, slightly arched at the nape, running cleanly into the shoulders, carried well up, giving the dog an alert, defiant appearance.*

Forequarters *Muscular, with deep chest. Shoulder blades should be long and broad, set obliquely and lying firmly on well-developed ribs. The breast bone should be prominent, extending so far forward as to show depressions on both*

sides. Upper arm equal in length to the shoulder blade, which it should join at an angle of 90 degrees, well boned and muscled, set on close to the ribs but moving freely. Lower arm short, inclined slightly inwards, well boned and free from wrinkle.

Body Long and well muscled with oblique shoulders and short strong pelvic region. Ribs well-sprung and extending far back. Chest oval, well let down between the forelegs, with the deepest point of the keel level with the wrist-joints. The line of the back level or only slightly depressed over the shoulders and slightly arched over the loin, with the belly moderately tucked up.

Hindquarters *Rump full, round and broad. Pelvic bone not too short, broad, strong and set obliquely. Thigh bone strong, of good length and jointed to the pelvis at an angle of 90 degrees. Second thighs short, set at right angles to the upper thigh and well muscled. Hocks well let down, set wide apart, strongly bent. Seen from behind the legs should be straight, with no tendency for the hocks to turn inwards or outwards.*

Feet *Broad and large in proportion to the size of the dog, straight or turned only slightly outwards. The hind feet smaller than the fore. Toes close together and with each toe well arched. Nails strong. The dog must stand equally on all parts of the foot.*

Tail *Set on fairly high, not too long, tapering and without too marked a curve. It should not be carried too high and never curled over the back.*

Coat *The coat should be soft and straight or only slightly waved. It is longest under the neck, on the under-parts of the body and behind the legs, where it should form abundant feathering and on the tail where it should form a flag. The outside of the ears should also be well feathered. The coat should be flat, resembling that of an Irish Setter, and should not obscure the outline. Too much hair on the feet is not desired.*

Colour *Any colour. No white is permissible except for a small spot on the breast and even this is undesirable. The nose should be black except in Dapples and Chocolates in which it may be flesh-coloured or brown. In all cases the coat colour should be bright and clearly defined. In black and tans the tan should be rich and sharp. Dapples should be free from large unbroken patches, the dappling being evenly distributed over the whole body.*

Weight and Size *The ideal weight is 10lb. (4.54kg.) and it is of the utmost importance that judges should not award a prize to any dog exceeding 11lb. (4.99kg.) in weight. Other points being equal the smaller the better, but mere diminutiveness must never take precedence over general type and soundness. Any appearance of weediness or toyishness is to be avoided at all costs.*

Faults *Round skull. Round or protruding eyes. Short ears.*

Shallow chest. Narrowness in front or behind. Short body. Long legs. Splayed feet. Cow hocks. Mouth under or overshot. Nervous or cringing demeanour.

Note *Male animals should have two apparently normal testicles fully descended into the scrotum.*

Miniature Smooth-haired
The Standard of the Dachshund (Miniature Smooth-haired) is identical with the Standard of the Dachshund (Miniature Long-haired) with the following exceptions:

Coat *In Smooths, short, dense and smooth, adequately covering all the parts of the body; coarsest on the under-side of the tail.*

Weight and Size *The ideal weight is 10lb. (4.54kg.) and it is of the utmost importance that judges should not award a prize to any dog exceeding 11lb. (4.99kg.) in weight. Other points being equal the smaller the better, but mere diminutiveness must never take precedence over general type and soundness. Any appearance of weediness or toyishness is to be avoided at all costs.*

Faults *Woolly or curly coat.*

Miniature Wire-haired
The Standard of the Dachshund (Miniature Wire-haired) is identical with the Standard of the Dachshund (Miniature Long-haired) with the following exceptions:

Coat *With the exception of the jaw, eyebrows and ears, the whole body is covered with a completely even, short, harsh coat and undercoat. There should be a beard on the chin. The eyebrows are bushy. The hair on the ears is almost smooth.*

Weight and Size *The ideal weight is 10lb. (4.54kg.) and it is of the utmost importance that judges should not award a prize to any dog exceeding 11lb. (4.99kg.) in weight. Other points being equal the smaller the better, but mere diminutiveness must never take precedence over general type and soundness. Any appearance of weediness or toyishness is to be avoided at all costs.*

The American Kennel Club Standard for The Dachshund
Summary
General Appearance *Short-legged, long-bodied, low-to-ground; sturdy, well muscled, neither clumsy nor slim, with*

audacious carriage and intelligent expression, conformation pre-eminently fitted for following game into burrows.

Head *Long, uniformly tapered, clean-cut; teeth well fitted, with scissors bite; eyes medium oval; ears broad, long, rounded, set on high and well back; neck long, muscular.* **Forequarters** *Muscular, compact. Chest deep, long, full and oval; breast-bone prominent. Broad, long shoulder, and oblique humerus forming right angle; heavy, set close; forearm short, inclined slightly in. Foreleg straight and vertical in profile, covering deepest point of chest. Feet broad, firm, compact, turned slightly out.* **Hindquarters** *Well-muscled and rounded. Pelvis, femur and tibia oblique, forming right angles; tarsus inclined forward. Hip should be level with shoulder, back strong, neither sagged nor more than very slightly arched. Tail strong, tapered, well-covered with hair, not carried gaily.*

Varieties *Three coat types: Smooth or Shorthaired, short and dense, shining, glossy. Wirehaired, like German Wirehaired Pointer, hard, with good undercoat. Longhaired, like Irish Setter.*

Note *In each coat variety there are divisions of open classes restricted to Miniatures, under 9lb. (4kg.), minimum age twelve months.*

Color *Solid red (tan) of various shades, and black with tan points, should have black noses and nails, and narrow black line edging lips and eyelids; chocolate with tan points permits brown nose. Eyes of all, lustrous, the darker the better.*

Faults *Overshot or undershot, knuckling over, loose shoulders; high on legs, clumsy gait, long, splayed or twisted feet, sagged or roached back, high croup, small, narrow or short chest, faulty angulation of fore or hindquarters, weak loins, narrow hindquarters, bowed legs, cowhocks, weak or dish-faced muzzle, dewlaps, uneven or scanty coat.*

General Features

General Appearance *Low to ground, short-legged, long-bodied, but with compact figure and robust muscular development; with bold and confident carriage of the head and intelligent facial expression. In spite of his shortness of leg, in comparison with his length of trunk, he should appear neither crippled, awkward, cramped in his capacity for movement, nor slim or weasel-like.*

Qualities *He should be clever, lively, and courageous to the* *point of rashness, persevering in his work both above and below ground; with all the senses well developed. His build and disposition qualify him especially for hunting game below ground. Added to this, his hunting spirit, good nose, loud tongue, and small size, render him especially suited for beating the bush. His figure and fine nose give him an especial advantage over most other breeds of sporting dogs for trailing.*

Conformation of Body

Head *Viewed from above or from the side, it should taper uniformly to the tip of the nose, and should be clean-cut. The skull is only slightly arched, and should slope gradually without stop (the less stop the more typical) into the finely-formed slightly-arched muzzle (ram's nose). The bridge bones over the eyes should be strongly prominent. The nasal cartilage and tip of the nose are long and narrow; lips tightly stretched, well covering the lower jaw, but neither deep nor pointed; corners of the mouth not very marked. Nostrils well open. Jaws opening wide and hinged well back of the eyes, with strongly developed bones and teeth.*

(a) Teeth: Powerful canine teeth should fit closely together, and the outer side of the lower incisors should tightly touch the inner side of the upper (scissors bite).

(b) Eyes: Medium size, oval, situated at the sides, with a clean, energetic, though pleasant expression; not piercing. Color, lustrous dark reddish-brown to brownish-black for all coats and colors. Wall (fish or pearl) eyes in the case of grey or dapple-colored dogs are not a very bad fault, but are also not desirable.

(c) Ears: Should be set near the top of the head, and not too far forward, long but not too long, beautifully rounded, not narrow, pointed or folded. Their carriage should be animated, and the forward edge should just touch the cheek.

(d) Neck: Fairly long, muscular, clean-cut, not showing any dewlap on the throat, slightly arched in the nape, extending in a graceful line into the shoulders, carried proudly but not stiffly.

Front *To endure the arduous exertion underground, the front must be correspondingly muscular, compact, deep, long and broad. Forequarters in detail:*

(a) Shoulder Blade: Long, broad, obliquely and firmly placed

Structural faults

Shoulder too forward

Roach-backed, short keel

Dipping back, shallow keel

Rear

Correct   Cow-hocked   Bow-legged

Front

Correct   Out at elbows   Crooked forelegs
                                                Out-turning feet

Angles of articulation with positions of the shoulder and pelvic girdle bones

1. Shoulder blade   2. Upper arm   3. Lower arm   4. Pelvis
5. Upper thigh (Femur)   6. Lower thigh (Tibia)   7. Tarsals

upon the fully developed thorax, furnished with hard and plastic muscles.

(b) Upper Arm: Of the same length as the shoulder blade, and at right angles to the latter, strong of bone and hard of muscle, lying close to the ribs, capable of free movement.

(c) Forearm: This is short in comparison to other breeds, slightly turned inwards; supplied with hard but plastic muscles on the front and outside, with tightly stretched tendons on the inside and at the back.

(d) Joint between forearm and foot (wrists): These are closer together than the shoulder joints, so that the front does not appear absolutely straight.

(e) Paws: Full, broad in front, and a trifle inclined outwards; compact, with well-arched toes and tough pads.

(f) Toes: There are five of these, though only four are in use. They should be close together, with a pronounced arch; provided on top with strong nails, and underneath with tough toe-pads.

Trunk *The whole trunk should in general be long and fully muscled. The back, with sloping shoulders, and short, rigid pelvis, should lie in the straightest possible line between the withers and the very slightly arched loins, these latter being short, rigid, and broad.*

(a) Chest: The breastbone should be strong, and so prominent in front that on either side a depression (dimple) appears. When viewed from the front, the thorax should appear oval, and should extend downwards to the mid-point of the forearm. The enclosing structure of ribs should appear full and oval, and when viewed from above or the side, full-volumed, so as to allow by its ample capacity, complete development of heart and lungs. Well ribbed up, and gradually merging into the line of the abdomen. If the length is correct, and also the anatomy of the shoulder and upper arm, the front leg when viewed in profile should cover the lowest point of the breast bone.

(b) Abdomen: Slightly drawn up.

Hindquarters *The hindquarters viewed from behind should be of completely equal width.*

(a) Croup: Long, round, full, robustly muscled, but plastic, only sinking slightly toward the tail.

(b) Pelvic Bones: Not too short, rather strongly developed, and moderately sloping.

(c) Thigh Bone: Robust and of good length, set at right angles to the pelvic bones.

(d) Hind Legs: Robust and well-muscled, with well-rounded buttocks.

(e) Knee Joint: Broad and strong.

(f) Calf Bone: In comparison with other breeds, short; it should be perpendicular to the thigh bone, and firmly muscled.

(g) The bones at the base of the foot (tarsus) should present a flat appearance, with a strongly prominent hock and a broad tendon of Achilles.

(h) The central foot bones (metatarsus) should be long, movable towards the calf bone, slightly bent toward the front, but perpendicular (as viewed from behind).

(i) Hind Paws: Four compactly closed and beautifully arched toes, as in the case of the front paws. The whole foot should be posed equally on the ball and not merely on the toes; nails short.

Tail *Set in continuation of the spine, extending without very pronounced curvature, and should not be carried too gaily.*

Note *Inasmuch as the Dachshund is a hunting dog, scars from honorable wounds shall not be considered a fault.*

Skeleton of the Dachshund

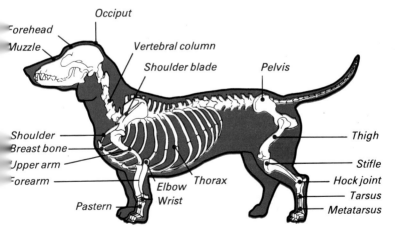

Occiput

Forehead

Muzzle

Vertebral column

Shoulder blade

Pelvis

Shoulder

Breast bone

Upper arm

Forearm

Pastern

Elbow

Wrist

Thorax

Thigh

Stifle

Hock joint

Tarsus

Metatarsus

Special Characteristics of the Three Coat-varieties

The Dachshund is bred with three varieties of coat: (1) Shorthaired (or Smooth); (2) Wirehaired; (3) Longhaired. All three varieties should conform to the characteristics already specified. The longhaired and shorthaired are old, well-fixed varieties, but into the wirehaired Dachshund, the blood of other breeds has been purposely introduced; nevertheless, in breeding him, the greatest stress must be placed upon conformity to the general Dachshund type. The following specifications are applicable separately to the three coat-varieties respectively:

(1) Shorthaired (or Smooth) Dachshund

Hair *Short, thick, smooth and shining; no bald patches. Special faults are: Too fine or thin hair, leathery ears, bald patches, too coarse or too thick hair in general. Tail: Gradually tapered to a point, well but not too richly haired; long, sleek bristles on the underside are considered a patch of strong-growing hair, not a fault. A brush tail is a fault, as is also a partly or wholly hairless tail.*

Color of hair, nose and nails *(a) One-colored Dachshund – This group includes red (often called tan), red-yellow, and yellow, with or without a shading of interspersed black hairs. Nevertheless a clean color is preferable, and red is to be considered more desirable than red-yellow or yellow. Dogs strongly shaded with interspersed black hairs belong to this class, and not to the other color groups. No white is desirable, but a solitary small spot is not exactly disqualifying. Nose and Nails – Black; red is admissible, but not desirable.*

(b) Two-colored Dachshund – These comprise deep black, chocolate, gray, and white; each with rust-brown or yellow marks over the eyes, on the sides of the jaw and underlip, on the inner edge of the ear, front, breast, inside and behind the front leg, on the paws and around the anus, and from there to about one-third to one-half of the length of the tail on the under side. (The most common two-colored Dachshund is usually called black-and-tan.) Except on white dogs, no white is desirable, but a solitary small spot is not exactly disqualifying. Absence, or undue prominence of tan markings is undesirable. Nose and Nails – In the case of black dogs, black; for chocolate, brown or gray; gray or even flesh color, but the last named color is not desirable; in the case of white dogs, black nose and

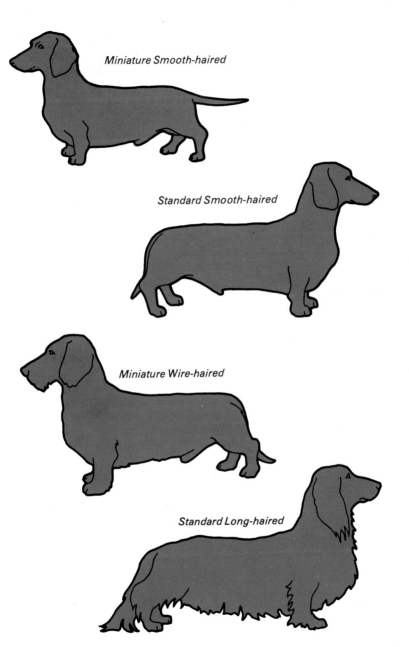

Miniature Smooth-haired

Standard Smooth-haired

Miniature Wire-haired

Standard Long-haired

35

nails are to be preferred.

(c) *Dappled and Striped Dachshund* — The color of the dappled (or tiger) Dachshund is a clear brownish or grayish color, or even a white ground, with dark irregular patches of dark-gray, brown, red-yellow or black (large areas of one color not desirable). It is desirable that neither the light nor the dark color should predominate. The color of the striped (brindle) Dachshund is red or yellow with a darker streaking. Nose and Nails — As for One- and Two-colored Dachshund.

(2) Wirehaired Dachshund

The general appearance is the same as that of the shorthaired, but without being long in the legs, it is permissible for the body to be somewhat higher off the ground.

Hair With the exception of jaw, eyebrows, and ears, the whole body is covered with a perfectly uniform tight, short, thick, rough, hard coat, but with finer, shorter hairs (undercoat) everywhere distributed between the coarser hairs, resembling the coat of the German Wirehaired Pointer. There should be a beard on the chin. The eyebrows are bushy. On the ears the hair is shorter than on the body, almost smooth, but in any case conforming to the rest of the coat. The general arrangement of the hair should be such that the wirehaired Dachshund, when seen from a distance should resemble the smoothhaired.

Any sort of soft hair in the coat is faulty, whether short or long, or wherever found on the body; the same is true of long, curly, or wavy hair, or hair that sticks out irregularly in all directions; a flag tail is also objectionable.

Tail: Robust, as thickly haired as possible, gradually coming to a point, and without a tuft.

Color of Hair, Nose and Nails All colors are admissible. White patches on the chest, though allowable, are not desirable.

(3) Longhaired Dachshund

The distinctive characteristic differentiating this coat from the shorthaired, or smoothhaired Dachshund is alone the rather long silky hair.

Hair The soft, sleek, glistening, often slightly wavy hair should be longer under the neck, on the underside of the body, and especially on the ears and behind the legs, becoming there a pronounced feather; the hair should attain its greatest length on the underside of the tail. The hair should fall beyond the lower edge of the ear. Short hair on the ear, so-called 'leather' ears, is not desirable. Too luxurious a coat causes the longhaired Dachshund to seem coarse, and masks the type. The coat should remind one of the Irish Setter, and should give the dog an elegant appearance. Too thick hair on the paws, so-called 'mops', is inelegant, and renders the animal unfit for use. It is faulty for the dog to have equally long hair over all the body, or if the coat is too curly, or too scrubby, or if a flag tail or overhanging hair on the ears are lacking; or if there is a very pronounced parting on the back, or a vigorous growth between the toes.

Tail: Carried gracefully in prolongation of the spine, the hair attains here its greatest length and forms a veritable flag.

Color of Hair, Nose and Nails: *Exactly as for the smoothhaired Dachshund.*

Note *Miniature Dachshunds are bred in all three coats. They are not undersized or undeveloped specimens of full-size Dachshunds, but have been purposely produced to work in burrows smaller than standard Dachshunds can enter. The limits set upon their size have inevitably resulted in a more slender body structure. Depth of chest and shortness of leg proportionate to the regular conformation would, in these diminutive animals, prove impractical for their active hunting purposes.*

The German specifications limit Zwergteckel (dwarf Dachshund) to a chest circumference of 13.8in. (35cm.), and limit Kaninchenteckel (rabbit Dachshund) to a chest circumference of 11.8in. (29.5cm.), certified at a minimum age of twelve months. Rather than the ideal, these sizes represent instead the upper limit for miniature re-registration; and thus in pedigrees provide an index to purity of miniature breeding.

In the United States Miniature Dachshunds have not been given separate classification. At American shows, a division of the open class for 'under nine pounds and twelve months old or over' permits class competition as miniatures, and opportunity in winners' classes to compete for championship points in each coat variety. Within the limits imposed, symmetrical adherence to the general Dachshund conformation, combined with smallness, and mental and physical vitality should be outstanding characteristics of the Miniature Dachshund.

General Faults
Serious Faults (which may prevent a dog from receiving any show rating): Overshot or undershot jaws, knuckling over, very loose shoulders.

Secondary Faults (which may prevent a dog from receiving a high show rating): A weak, long-legged, or dragging figure; body hanging between the shoulders; sluggish, clumsy, or waddling gait; toes turned inwards or too obliquely outwards; splayed paws; sunken back, roach (or carp) back; croup higher than withers; short-ribbed or too weak chest; excessively drawn-up flanks like those of a Greyhound; narrow, poorly muscled hindquarters; weak loins; bad angulation in front or hindquarters; cowhocks; bowed legs; 'glass' eyes, except for gray or dappled dogs; a bad coat.

Minor Faults (which may prevent a dog from receiving the highest rating in championship competition): Ears wrongly set, sticking out, narrow or folded; too marked a stop; too pointed or weak a jaw; pincer teeth, distemper teeth; too wide or too short a head; goggle eyes, 'glass' eyes in the case of gray or dappled dogs, insufficiently dark eyes in the case of all other coat-colors; dewlaps; short neck; swan neck; too fine or too thin hair.

It is interesting to compare the slight but significant differences between the American and British Dachshund standards, differences which have led to a divergence of winning types on either side of the Atlantic. American standard Dachshunds tend to be bigger than their British counterparts and differ in head qualities and the degree of straightness desired in the front legs. Conversely, American Miniature Dachshunds are required to be smaller than those acceptable in the British show ring.

A brace of Smooth-haired Dachshunds

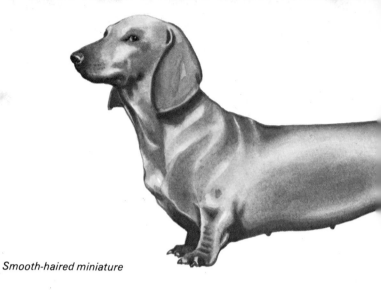

Smooth-haired miniature

(These are not in correct size relationship)

Smooth-haired standard

41

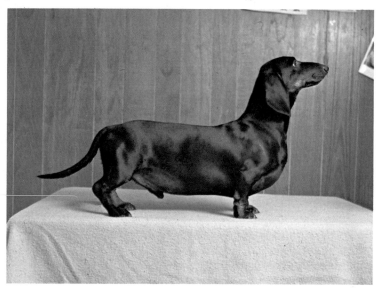

Smooth-haired standard Dachshund

Smooth-haired miniature Dachshund

42

Smooth-haired standard Dachshunds, one dog and two bitches

Wire-haired standard Dachshund

Wire-haired miniature Dachshund

44

Long-haired standard Dachshund

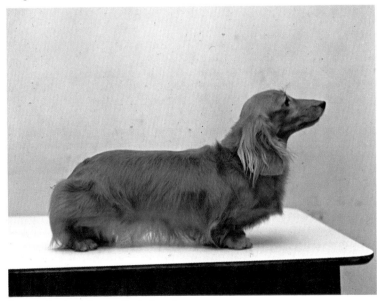

Long-haired miniature Dachshund

Choosing a puppy

When you have decided the size and coat of Dachshund that you wish to own, the choice of breeder is of the utmost importance. You will be acquiring a puppy which will become part of your life for anything up to fifteen years and therefore it should have had the very best of rearing and care to lay the foundations for a strong, healthy and lively dog.

Puppies can be purchased either from an owner with only one bitch who has the occasional litter, or from a well known breeder who usually runs a kennel of show dogs. If you have the chance, view as many litters as you can before making your final choice. This will give you a much better insight into the breed.

When choosing a puppy ask to see the mother as well as the litter mates. The father may well not be owned by the breeder so you are unlikely to be able to see him. Watch the puppies playing and ask if you can pick them up. Feel the coat and see that it is not dry and scurfy. The eyes should look bright and alert with no discharge. The puppies should look well rounded and not thin or pot-bellied. Avoid the nervous puppy who hides in a corner. Puppies should be bold and friendly, though not all litters are exposed to the same amount of human contact so, when confronted with a mass of people, some may take more time to adjust to the situation.

As a prospective owner you should feel free to ask all the questions you want. A conscientious breeder is only too happy to give the benefits of his experience in the breed.

There are a large number of breed societies catering for Dachshund enthusiasts. Addresses of these can be obtained from the Kennel Club and the secretaries of these breed clubs are always willing to put prospective owners in touch with the nearest breeder of the dog of their choice. There are a number of publications which also list breeders and puppies for sale. These are listed at the back of this book.

The pet owner who breeds a litter will usually advertise in the local paper, and one of the best ways of all of finding the right breeder is through the recommendation of another owner.

The permissible colours for a Smooth-haired Dachshund are listed in the Standard, but the commonest colours are red or black-and-tan. If you want a chocolate or dapple Dachshund

Smooth-haired mother with litter

you may have to search for quite a long while. The puppy's coat at eight weeks should be smooth and glossy, though the Smooths are liable to get bald patches on the chest and ears at about this age. This is often referred to as 'milk rash' and soon clears up. The application of benzyl benzoate, obtainable from chemists, is often a great help.

The Long-haired puppy comes in the same colour range as the Smooth. Here the coat at eight weeks is soft and fluffy with the beginnings of the longer hair on the top of the ears and on the hind legs and tail.

The commonest colour in the Wire-haired Dachshund is brindle of various shades. The coat of an eight-week-old Wire puppy does differ from puppy to puppy. Some look fluffy all over with the beginnings of bushy eyebrows and beard. These are most appealing but when adult will require stripping frequently. Otherwise they will tend to look like door mats and will become over-heated in the summer. Other puppies, within the same litter, will just have started to grow the longer hairs on the body and some wispy hairs around the mouth and eyebrows. This type of puppy coat will become a good, harsh, adult jacket which will require only occasional stripping. The third type is the one that looks like a smooth but the coat texture is thicker. Careful examination will reveal a few long or guard hairs on parts of the body or down the legs. It can take up to four months of age before the real signs of wire coat become apparent. It is this last type of coat that will become the wire coat described as ideal in the Standard, and it is much sought after in the show ring.

If you want a dog for showing then it is advisable to visit a few shows and speak to breeders there. Again the dog magazines will tell you when and where the nearest shows are to be held. Note the kennels which seem to produce the winning stock and go to them for advice. Never be afraid to ask questions. If a breeder knows that you want a puppy for show then he or she will try to pick out the most promising for you.

It is always a gamble picking a show puppy at eight weeks but some obvious faults will be apparent at that age. A puppy with a bad mouth, either overshot or undershot, or with incorrect pigment on the nose is clearly of pet quality only. The same goes for very fluffy Wire-haired puppies. Sadly, even the most promising puppy does not always mature into a first rate show specimen, so do not expect any breeder to guarantee you a show-winning animal.

A Wire-haired pet

General care

The ideal time for a Dachshund puppy to go to its new home is at eight weeks of age. By this time it will have been weaned and will be ready to face the outside world. For the first two months of life it has been dependent not only on its mother but also on its litter mates to provide the stimulation needed to grow into a well adjusted puppy that will, under the right care and conditions, become the ideal family pet.

The first few days in a new home can be traumatic for a puppy. It will be surrounded by strange smells, strange people and strange objects and will be missing the company of the rest of the litter. A puppy's memory is, however, short. Provided it is carefully introduced to new experiences so that it does not find them frightening, it will adjust to its new life and routine without too much difficulty.

It is during the night that the new puppy will feel most lost, and you must be prepared for a few sleepless nights with the puppy crying. Some never make a murmur right from the day that they first go to their new homes, but these are rather the exception. With a Dachshund puppy you must try and be firm enough to endure the first few disturbed nights. It will soon grow out of the habit but once you give in and take the puppy to bed with you, you are lost. Any Dachshund given the chance will prefer to sleep in your bed rather than its own, which is both unhygienic and not very restful for the human occupant. Play with the puppy just before bedtime to tire it, give the last milky feed of the day and make sure that its bed is in a warm, draughtproof area with plenty of blankets. Close the door and make a resolution that you will not go back to the puppy until the morning.

Feeding The breeder should provide the new owner with a diet sheet, so do not hesitate to ask for one. If possible try to give the puppy exactly the kind of food it has been used to, for the reaction to changing homes can cause slight stomach upsets which could be aggravated by changing the diet too much. All food changes should be introduced gradually into a dog's diet anyway.

At eight weeks of age the puppy will be on four feeds per day; two meat and biscuit meal, and two milky feeds. This is continued until about four months when one milk feed is cut out with the amount of meat increased according to need.

Once the dog is fully grown it can have either one main meal or two smaller feeds a day.

Suggested diet for puppies (amounts for Miniatures in brackets)

Breakfast: about 4oz. or 113g. (2oz. or 57g.) warm milk thickened with a baby cereal or brown bread. Once or twice a week add raw egg yolk or a whole scrambled egg.

Lunch: about 4oz. or 113g. (2oz. or 57g.) raw or cooked meat mixed with a tablespoon (dessertspoon) of soaked puppy biscuit meal. Add a vitamin powder according to the directions on the container.

Supper: as lunch. *Bedtime:* as breakfast.

Increase the meat until by the age of a year the puppy is having about 10-12oz. or 284-340g. (6-8oz. or 170-227g.) per day with biscuit meal increased as required. Not all puppies or full grown dogs require the same amount of food to keep them in good condition. The best guide as to whether the puppy or adult is having enough to eat is the look of the animal. Is the coat shiny, the body well filled out? It should not be so fat as to wobble or so thin that the ribs show. The dog should look well rounded with a slight waist. The feeding of a Dachshund, especially a standard, is important for although it is a short-legged breed it has a large frame and heavy bone to maintain. However, once the growing stage has passed, great care must be taken not to allow the Dachshund to become too fat. Dachshunds are usually excessively greedy and become overweight very easily. There is nothing more pitiful than seeing a fat Dachshund that can hardly walk and whose stomach almost touches the ground. Because of this tendency to obesity, titbits should never be given.

There are many different types of food on the market from fresh or tinned meat to complete dry foods. Whichever you choose be guided by the breeder or dog food supplier. In most areas there are kennels supplying dog food on a cash and carry basis which can help cut the costs. Also by going to people who supply these different types of food, you will ensure that your puppy has a varied diet.

The puppy will need two dishes, one for water which must always be available and fresh daily, and the other for food. It is advisable not to have plastic as these nearly always get chewed. China is not always a good idea as some puppies like to pick their dishes up and crash them around. Oblong or

Suitable metal feeding dishes

round pie dishes and cake tins make useful dog dishes. Feeding utensils must be kept clean. Any uneaten food should not be left on the ground, especially in summer when it can easily become flyblown. Never give your Dachshund bones that can splinter, such as chop or poultry bones. Large marrow bones may be given at any age. They will keep the dog occupied for hours and are especially useful when the puppy is at the chewing and destructive stage.

Housing A Dachshund is a house pet. It loves its home comforts and should not be kept out in a kennel unless you are planning on keeping a number for breeding. The Smooth-haired especially feels the cold and, given half the chance, likes nothing better than sleeping under the eiderdown or even inside the bed. Dachshunds are gregarious and, when several are kept together, one bed is usually sufficient as all will pile in on top of each other, even into the smallest of spaces. Non-Dachshund friends are amazed to see a basket full of

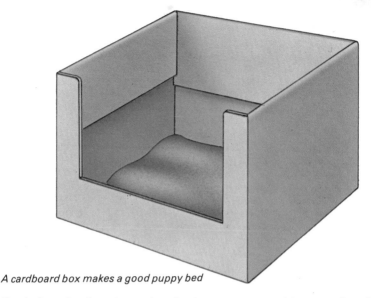

A cardboard box makes a good puppy bed

Dachshunds, heads and tails interwoven, with sounds of heavy breathing and the occasional grunts from the dog right at the bottom. One can hardly believe that they will not all suffocate but this is how Dachshunds love to sleep, no doubt partly because of their instincts of going to ground in the hunting field.

Young puppies are great chewers and for this reason it is inadvisable to buy an expensive bed until you are sure they have grown out of the habit, or at least are not quite so destructive. A large cardboard box provides an ideal bed which can be renewed when necessary without any expense. Place the box in a draught-free corner of the kitchen or wherever you want the puppy to sleep. Choose a position where the pup can find peace and quiet but still feel it is with the family. Puppies need lots of rest and should be left undisturbed to sleep as much as they wish.

The bedding, which should be changed and washed regularly, can be of old blankets. Care should be taken that any holes, either made by wear or by the puppy itself, are not of such a size that the pup can get stuck in any way. If you use old clothes, jumpers, coats, etc., cut the seams so as to open out the sleeves. These are another hazard not often considered.

Marrow bones are useful for a pet to chew upon

I know of at least two accidents happening, one of which ended in tragedy. One was when an adult Dachshund became stuck in the sleeve of a jumper and, in its panic to get free, fell into a lily pond and drowned. The other instance was of a puppy which got its head stuck in a Wellington boot. It was fortunate that the owner heard strange noises and found the puppy in time before it suffocated. Both puppies and adults are very like children. They are into everything new and the owner must always try to be one step ahead.

When you feel the puppy is ready for a permanent bed, there are various kinds on the market. There is the traditional cane basket which should be of a size in which the dog can lie stretched out. There are metal-framed beds with canvas bases and fitted covers, or there are hard-wearing plastic or wooden boxes. Perhaps the most suitable is the metal-framed type or the wooden box, as neither can be chewed very easily. All types of dog bed can be purchased from your local pet shop.

Outside kennelling for Dachshunds should be draughtproof and warm and constructed of either brick or wood which should be lined. In winter heating will be necessary, either infra-red lamps or similar electric heating which should, of course, be correctly installed and maintained. Never use

A wicker basket bed

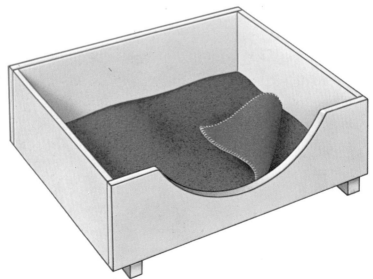

A home-made wooden bed with blanket

54

Hard-wearing plastic bed

paraffin stoves. However, it is only when quite a number of dogs are being considered that kennels should be necessary.

Exercising Dachshunds are a most adaptable breed as regards exercising. Whereas they are game to walk all day with you, they are equally happy with a short, regular daily walk, providing they have a garden in which to play. Dachshund puppies should not be taken for walks of any length until they are about six months of age. Once they have had their inoculations they are ready to meet other dogs and leave the confines of their gardens.

The puppy must first learn to wear a collar, and this can be done by letting it wear one around the house for a few days before attempting to attach the lead. The first few times using the collar and lead can be quite exhausting with the puppy rolling on its back or leaping about like a fish on a line. However, it will soon learn to accept the inevitable and this is the time to take short excursions out of the garden to get it used to traffic. This must be a gradual process. It is important for it to become used to meeting people and traffic, but the puppy should not be required to walk for any great distances for the first few months.

For the first collar, buy the cheapest you can, for the puppy will quickly outgrow it. It should be lightweight and so should the lead. For standard Dachshunds by the age of six months, a choke chain collar and a good strong leather lead with a metal clasp is essential. The Miniatures obviously need a lighter type. Leather collars for exercising are not a good idea. They stretch with use and a dog can quite easily wriggle its head out.

Basic training Dachshunds can be obstinate and occasionally wilfully disobedient. For this reason firm and consistent training should start as soon as you get your puppy. Do not expect too much from a baby but familiarise it with its name as soon as possible by making sure that its name is always associated with something pleasant such as a meal or a game. This is one of the few occasions when bribery is allowable for a very small tit bit when your puppy answers to its name will help you to establish the habit of coming when called. Praise is a powerful stimulant to behaving in a civilised manner. Neither puppies nor adults should be hit. They are very susceptible to correction by voice only, and a harsh tone can produce far more results than a smack. None of the hound breeds is suitable for obedience enthusiasts, as they are all too independently minded. Sensible correction for misdoings is all that is needed, for Dachshunds are highly intelligent and will do as they are told if only because they want to remain in your good books.

Wire-haired standard Dachshund

Kennel run showing a layout for multiple kennels

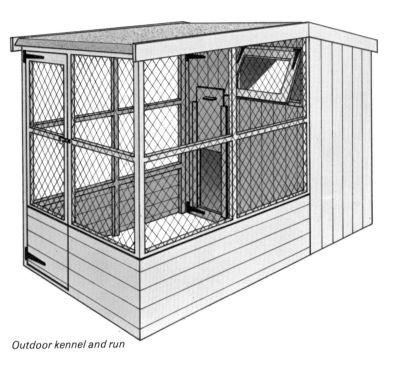

Outdoor kennel and run

They are usually quite easy to housetrain. Having a puppy in the summer months is a lot easier, as it can spend so much more time outside. Most puppies, when they go to their new homes, will have been trained to relieve themselves on newspaper and this should be put down at night for them in their new homes. A puppy will not be able to go all night without wetting until about four months.

During the day the puppy must be put outside as soon as it wakes up from a rest and after feeding and play. Stay with it until it performs and then praise the puppy lavishly. If you are vigilant enough to prevent mistakes occurring in the wrong place and praise the puppy lavishly for the right response, it will be very quick to learn. Once a puppy is housetrained, try not to leave it too long in the house without a chance of going out or you will undo all your good work.

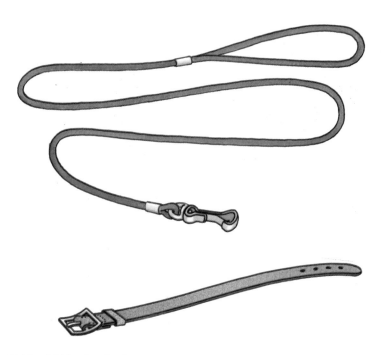

Lightweight lead and collar

Double slip collar

Grooming

One of the many points in favour of a Dachshund is their lack of doggy smell. They also require very little grooming in comparison with other breeds. All three coats are easy to maintain provided the diet is correct and the dog has enough exercise.

The Smooth-haired Dachshund has obviously the easiest of the three coats to groom. This only need be done once a week or so using a bristle brush or a hound glove. Finish off with a wipe over with a slightly damp chamois leather or even a piece of velvet and the animal will be in shining condition. Do not bath the dog unless you feel it is really necessary, when a good proprietary brand of dog shampoo should be used. Throughout life the Smooth is prone to bare patches, usually on the ears and down the chest, but sometimes on the back. Application of benzyl benzoate helps to stop these bare patches spreading and allows new coat growth. However, veterinary advice should always be sought if the baldness spreads.

Ears should be checked weekly for signs of canker or infection. Ear troubles can become chronic so, if the dog has red, sore ears, or any sort of discharge from the ear, it is wiser to seek professional help for treatment. The ear flaps can be cleaned gently with moist cotton wool, or cotton buds as sold for babies. Nothing should ever be poked down the ear canal itself. The edges of the leathers tend to become dry and encrusted in Smooth Dachshunds and an application of baby oil can help here.

The teeth of a young dog should not cause any trouble. Marrow bones and hard biscuits help to keep the teeth clean and prevent the formation of tartar which looks like a brown deposit on the tooth. Tartar tends to collect round the roots of the canine teeth and if left causes the gums to recede and finally the tooth to decay. With a tractable dog, tartar can be removed by the owner with a tooth scaler. Very often bad breath in an old dog is caused by dirty teeth.

Nails on some dogs need constant attention. They should not be allowed to become too long as this affects movement. A Dachshund with the correct shaped foot will need very little attention providing it has concrete to walk on or a certain amount of road walking. Nails can be cut with clippers but

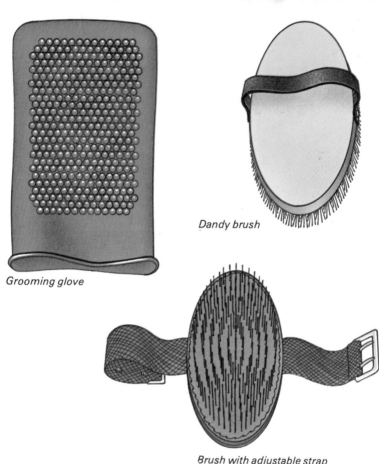

Grooming glove

Dandy brush

Brush with adjustable strap

Oval bristle brush

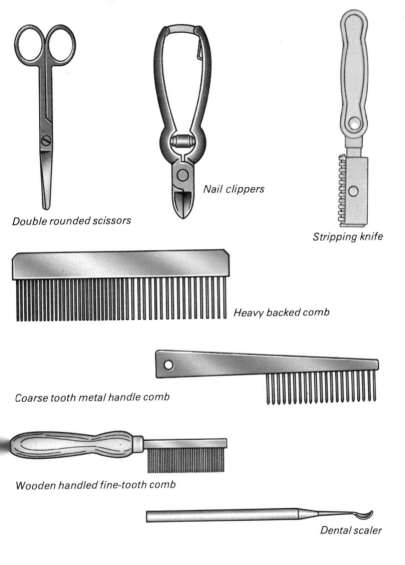

Double rounded scissors

Nail clippers

Stripping knife

Heavy backed comb

Coarse tooth metal handle comb

Wooden handled fine-tooth comb

Dental scaler

There are many useful items that can be purchased for grooming the particular coat type that you own

great care must be taken to remove only a little at a time. Each nail has a living quick of blood vessels and nerves growing down inside it. In a white nail this can be seen as a pink line down the centre but with the dark nails common in Dachshunds this is not possible. Should the quick be accidentally cut it will bleed and cause the dog great pain. Some people find it easier to file the end of the nail to a slightly curved hook which then wears down more quickly. Do not forget to check the dewclaws on the front legs for overgrowth.

While grooming, check that there are no fleas or lice present on the dog. Fleas can be noticed when the coat is brushed the wrong way. A brown, scurrying insect is almost certainly a flea. Also look for the small black specks on the skin which are flea excreta. Lice are a little more difficult to notice, as they do not move but remain attached to the skin where they suck their host's blood. They are round insects, often swollen and dark in colour. Do not pull them off without first loosening their hold on the dog by dabbing them with an astringent such as methylated spirit. The lice eggs are found along the hairs and might be mistaken for scurf, the only difference being that scurf can be brushed off the coat but the eggs remain attached to the hair. If livestock are found, the dog should be thoroughly powdered with a flea powder, not forgetting to treat its bed and surroundings. Alternatively, bath the dog in an insecticidal shampoo.

Show preparation for a Smooth Dachshund is minimal. Providing it is regularly groomed with ears, teeth, and nails checked, and is generally fit, all that is needed on the day of the show is a final polish with a soft cloth.

A little more grooming is required to keep the Long-haired Dachshund's coat in condition. The ear, tail and back feathering can mat unless regularly brushed and combed. Use a bristle brush and a fairly wide toothed steel comb. Grooming is easier if you train your dog to stand on a table. This is simply a matter of patience when the dog is young, but do make sure the table has a non-slip surface. A rubber bath mat makes a good covering.

The only parts of the Long-hair which need trimming are the feet. Use blunt-nosed scissors to remove the long hairs between the toes and under the pads and to give a neatly rounded appearance to the foot. Unless this is done, mud balls can form under the pads in wet weather, making walking difficult. General care is as for the Smooth-haired variety.

It is a good idea to bath your Long-haired Dachshund before a show to give the coat a really glossy appearance. If your Long-hair has rather a curly coat, it should be bathed at least a week before the show to allow the coat to settle. Brushing the coat as it dries helps to reduce the waviness. If the coat is the correct flat coat, then two days before the show is about right for bathing. Make sure that you have trimmed the feet correctly and that the dog is in sparkling condition.

The Wire-haired coat needs stripping at intervals as well as regular grooming and general care. The correct wire coat, as decribed in the Standard, needs very little attention, just tidying up round the face, tail and feet occasionally. Even this is not usually necessary for the pet Wire-hair. However, this type of coat is rare.

The softer and more heavily coated Wires do need stripping up to three times a year. This means taking the top coat off to expose the undercoat. The best method is by using finger and thumb to pluck out the longer, harsher top coat. However, it is quicker to use a stripping knife and this is the most usual way of trimming pet Wires. The top coat is taken off the body, head and legs, leaving on the beard, bushy eyebrows, and the feathering down the legs and on the chest bone. When the new coat grows through, which can take up to eight weeks, an overall harsh wire jacket becomes apparent.

Most breeders will have their puppies back for stripping, or the owner can learn to do this for himself. If you want to learn, try to watch someone else doing the job first, as this will teach you far more than words. It is a great help for novices to have a photograph of a correctly trimmed Wire to which they can refer. Remember that the photograph shows you a dog with the new coat grown through, but it will indicate the areas that are left untouched. A mirror behind the dog you are stripping will help you achieve an even effect on both sides. Proficiency comes with experience in this as in most aspects of dog care.

Dog beauty parlours will also strip pet Wires but do not rely on them being very familiar with the breed. Take a photograph for them to look at, or you might get a dog back minus beard and eyebrows.

Show preparation for the Wire-haired Dachshund depends very much on the type of coat. The correct wire coat needs very little attention but the coat that needs stripping will have to be

Correctly trimmed Wire-haired Dachshund

done between four and eight weeks before the show to allow time for the new harsh hair to have grown through. A Wire-hair that has just been stripped and is only showing its undercoat should not be exhibited. The time limit for stripping your dog right out can be found out only through trial and error, as the new hair grows at a different rate on each individual animal.

Show preparation for the Miniature coats follows that of the standards. It must be remembered that there is a weight limit for Miniatures. If your Dachshund is near the limit it should be weighed regularly and the diet adjusted accordingly. Never on any account starve your Miniature if it is over the weight limit. It must have an adequate diet. Some do go over weight and for these the show ring is regrettably out.

Exhibiting and show training

Dog showing is not only for the experts. Any owner of a well bred dog can have great fun from attending local shows at first, and then progressing to the larger events.

In choosing your Dachshund you may already have decided that you wanted a show quality puppy and have been guided by the breeder into buying one that will hopefully be good enough. However, many puppies sold as pets mature into something worth showing. Do not hesitate to ask the breeder, or any other knowledgeable person, if your dog might be suitable. Or take it to some shows and find out that way.

In Britain there are various types of show from Exemption shows run for charity, through Sanction, Limited and Open shows, to the biggest of all, Championship shows. At the last mentioned, the very valued Challenge Certificates are on offer to some or all breeds. These are awarded to the best dog and the best bitch of the breed in question. To become a British champion a dog must win three of these under different judges at different shows.

In America show categories run from Matches to Speciality and Points shows, the last mentioned being where one can win points towards a championship status for one's dog. To become an American champion a dog must win a total of fifteen points and two of these wins must be 'majors' (three or more points won at the same show) won under different judges. The number of points awarded at a show depends on the number of dogs and bitches of the breed actually present and can also vary from area to area.

The definitions of classes at shows are totally different in Britain and America. All would-be exhibitors should obtain the show regulations from their respective Kennel Clubs and study them. However, in neither country can any dog be shown which is not Kennel Club registered. This is one of the reasons why it is so important to make sure that your puppy is registered when you buy it. It could be very disappointing to get the urge to show or breed and find that one's dog, though purebred, was ineligible.

Shows are advertised in the dog magazines. Write to the secretary running the show for a schedule and entry form. This must be filled in clearly and returned to the secretary before the closing date printed on it.

Table

"New" dogs (unseen by Judge)

Handler

Judge

Dog being examined by Judge

"Old" dogs (already seen by Judge in a previous class)

Table

Judge

All dogs

"Once round, please"

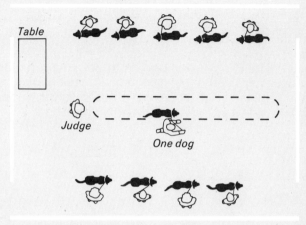

"Once up and down, please"

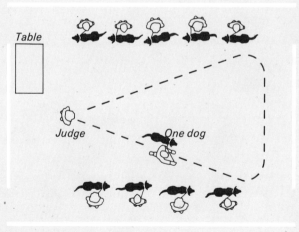

"Triangle, please"

Before attending your first show, try to find a local training class which teaches ringcraft. These classes will help you and your dog to learn what is expected of you both in the show ring. The dog will be taught to tolerate being handled by strangers and to walk round a ring full of other dogs without attempting to fight or play with them.

Dachshunds, when being shown, are required to stand on a table and be examined by the judge who will look at the mouth and run his hands over the body to check conformation and condition. After the the table examination, the handler has to move the dog round the ring for the judge to assess movement. When all the dogs in the class have been examined

American show stance for the Smooth-haired Dachshund

in this way, the dogs have to stand correctly in front of their owners for the judge to make his final decisions. Always keep your eye on the judge and follow his, and the steward's, directions. In judging Miniatures, once the final selection has been made, the prize winners have to go on the scales to make sure that they are not overweight.

As Dachshunds are judged on the table, it is essential that from an early age they become used to standing on one. This can be done quite easily by placing the dog four square on a table each day and letting it hold the position for a few seconds. A titbit on these occasions is justified. Be very careful that the dog does not become frightened or fall off, as this

Handler shows a Long-haired Dachshund in the American show ring

Judging is carried out with the dog on a table

could put it off showing for life. Also practise walking round with the dog on a loose lead. A few minutes a day is all that is necessary.

Bitches in season should not be taken to shows as it upsets any male dog, and could also lead to infection for the bitch.

Never exhibit a dog which shows even the slightest symptom of being unwell. It is not only very unfair to fellow exhibitors, it is also unfair to the dog itself.

The larger shows are very often benched, which means that all dogs entered for competition will have to stay on their bench for a good part of the day. It is therefore necessary to have a collar and a benching chain with which to fasten the dog. Benching chains have a clip at either end and one or two swivel links in the middle. These, and nylon show lead, are obtainable from the trade stands at the show. You should also take your grooming equipment, food for yourself and the dog, a water bowl and water, and a blanket for the dog to lie on. Some shows send out exhibitors' passes beforehand and you will need to remember to take this and a pin for pinning on your ring number card.

Benching chain

Transportation cage

73

Breeding

The myth that all bitches should have at least one litter has no credence today. Most Dachshunds make excellent mothers but the fact that a bitch has never had a litter does not affect her in any way.

Before breeding from your bitch it is wise to consider the following points. A litter is time consuming and costly to rear. What is the market like for puppies? You will be an unknown breeder and therefore could have difficulty in selling them. Do you have the facilities for housing a bitch and her litter?

A standard Dachshund can have up to eight puppies at a time. Inside accommodation is necessary for the whelping and for at least the first four weeks after the litter is born. Once they are old enough to go outside, a good sized kennel and run must be available.

Not all puppies will be sold by eight weeks of age and you may be forced to keep some until they are anything up to six months old.

The time of the year can be an important factor as well. Winter puppies will need extra heating and this adds to the overall cost of the litter. Also, if the weather is very bad, it may not be possible to put the puppies outside at all.

Finally, take a good hard look at your bitch. Is she a good enough specimen of the breed, both in conformation and temperament, to be bred from?

If, after considering these points, you still wish to go ahead and have a litter, then have the bitch examined by a veterinary surgeon to make sure that she is physically able to be bred and that she is in a healthy condition. Seek advice from the breeder as to the most suitable mate for her. Do not use the dog down the road just because he is convenient. As with the bitch, you want a stud who is a good representative of the breed and who has a good temperament.

If you are able, attend some shows where you will see the top stud dogs and their progeny. The experienced breeders will always be happy to advise which dog is most likely to suit your bitch.

Bitches come into season or 'on heat' at intervals varying from every six months to every ten months. A few are more frequent or may go even longer between seasons. A bitch should not be bred from until at least her second season, or

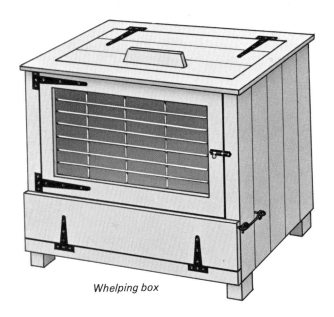

Whelping box

preferably her third, and should not be expected to have her first litter after the age of about five years.

Before the bitch comes into season at the time you want to mate her, you will have decided which dog to use and made a tentative booking with the stud dog owner. When the season starts, make a note of the date and advise the stud dog owner.

The conventional time to mate a Dachshund is between the eleventh and fourteenth day after the coloured discharge first starts to show. However, not all follow this pattern and the time can vary from the eighth to about the eighteenth day. The best guide is the bitch herself. She will curve her tail when touched at the rear end and will flirt with any other dog she meets, very often irrespective of its sex. The discharge from the vagina will turn from the bright red blood colour to an almost clear secretion while the vulva remains soft and swollen.

Be very careful that the bitch cannot get out or with any male dog. At this time most bitches have no scruples! Whether you are planning on mating your bitch or not, care must be taken for the three weeks she is in season. With so many stray dogs

Dog

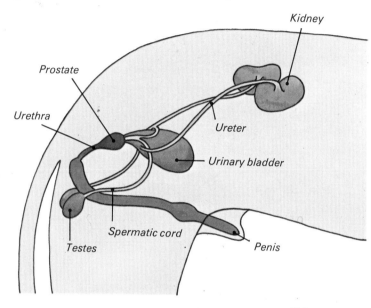

Bitch

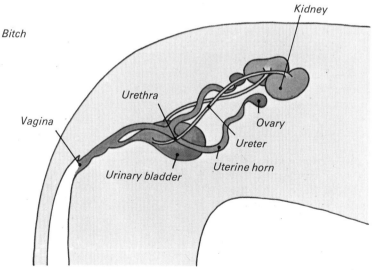

about, the males soon find any interesting bitch and they can become a real menace.

Never take your bitch in season out for a walk in the immediate vicinity of your home. Either leave her in the garden or else take her in the car for exercise on the lead away from home.

The bitch is as a rule taken to the stud dog. In some cases the stud dog owner will keep the bitch for a few days to ensure that she is mated at the correct time. The mating is done under supervision from the stud dog owner who helps the dog if necessary while the bitch's owner holds her head and gives her confidence.

A maiden bitch may feel rather apprehensive about the whole thing and, on occasions, try to snap at the dog. Provided the dog is an experienced stud, this will not put him off. The dog and bitch should be allowed to flirt and play before the mating as this will also help to give the bitch confidence. If possible a maiden bitch should return for a second mating, usually the next day or the one after, depending on the stud dog owner's recommendation.

It is important to organise the whelping quarters soon after the mating in order that the bitch can become used to the whelping box in good time. The box should be constructed of wood, preferably in sections to allow for easy cleaning, and of such a size as to allow the bitch to lie stretched out and turn round without any difficulty. On the inside there should be a narrow strip of wood right round the box about 6in. (15cm.) from the bottom. This is to help prevent the bitch from lying on the puppies as they can get underneath the bar and so out of her way. Start collecting newspapers as they are invaluable for lining the whelping box and also the puppy pen once the puppies start moving around.

The whelping room or area should be in a quiet part of the house that can easily be kept warm. The room temperature should be maintained at 70°F (21°C) during the first three weeks. As whelping very often takes place at night, a comfortable chair or even a camp bed will be appreciated by the person who sits up with the bitch.

The gestation time for a bitch is sixty-three days and for the first five to six weeks no special feeding or exercise are necessary, providing the bitch is fit and has a well balanced diet.

For the last weeks prior to whelping, the bitch must be given extra food and the exercise should be cut down, depending on how heavy she is becoming. The bitch will require about double the amount of her usual feed and the increase should be in the protein food and not the carbohydrates. The extra food must be split up into two or even three feeds daily, as a bitch carrying a large litter will not be able to take too much food at one time without becoming uncomfortable. Extra vitamins are recommended given according to the directions.

About a week before the expected date of arrival, take the bitch to the veterinary surgeon to have her checked that all is in order and to advise him as to the whelping date in case you have to call for his assistance. A bitch can whelp anytime between the fifty-eighth and sixty-fifth day, but if nothing has happened by this time professional advice must again be sought.

The following equipment should be got ready:

1. A bowl of disinfectant for washing your hands should you need to help.

2. A pair of sharp, surgical scissors with which to cut the puppy's umbilical cord should the mother fail to do this.

3. Clean, warm towels to dry the puppies if the mother will not.

4. Cotton wool.

5. A small box and a hot water bottle. If it is a large litter it is sometimes necessary to put the first-born pups in the box so that the bitch can concentrate on producing the remainder of the litter.

6. A puppy milk powder which can be used if the bitch's milk is slow in coming through. The bitch will enjoy drinking this herself anyway if the puppies do not need it.

Before the final phase is reached the bitch should have her stomach and rear parts sponged down with disinfectant, general grooming having been done as usual throughout pregnancy. The Long-haired bitch will need to have the hair cut from round her nipples and also a small amount from the tail and back featherings. This will help in keeping her clean after whelping. The Smooth-haired needs no special attention. It is a good idea to have the Wire stripped some weeks before whelping, then this variety will require just trimming under the stomach.

The following signs indicate that whelping is imminent,

Items required when preparing to deliver a litter

though different bitches have different behaviour patterns. The bitch may become restless, running from room to room and refusing food. She may seek a dark corner or start scratching in the whelping box. Her temperature will drop about two degrees. The normal temperature is 101.5°F (38.6°C) but for an accurate reading this has to be taken at the same time daily for a period.

There is a clear discharge from the vulva and the bitch starts having contractions. This heavy straining and heaving is the most important sign and the time this starts should be carefully noted, for if no puppy arrives in three hours, something may be amiss and veterinary advice must be sought. The three-hour period must be watched for after each arrival, as it is no guarantee that as one puppy has been delivered safely the others will arrive without any trouble.

A puppy is born enclosed in a tough membranous bag or sac. This must be broken as soon as the puppy emerges from the mother. Any delay could cause the puppy to drown in the fluid that has been protecting it while in its mother's womb.

A normal whelping requires the minimum of interference from the owner. You will just be present to give moral support and to watch that nothing goes wrong. A bitch's natural instincts will tell her exactly what to do as each puppy is born. It is possible, if a bitch is very heavy, that she will not be able to reach round to her rear end and in such a case the owner will have to help and break the bag to release the puppy. Occasionally a bitch, after expelling a puppy, will decline to have anything to do with it and again the owner must quickly attend to it. Once the bag is broken, the umbilical cord should be cut about an inch or so from the puppy's stomach.

If the bitch still shows no interest, the puppy must be dried with a towel, taking care to ensure that the nostrils and mouth are clear of fluid. The puppy can then be put back with the bitch who, attracted by the puppy's cries, will usually start to lick and nuzzle it.

With a large litter some pups can be put in a small box alongside the whelping bed until everything is over. If you have a very maternal bitch who is worried by this, it is better to keep her happy and risk leaving the puppies with her throughout.

Each puppy is attached to an afterbirth and this comes away either with the puppy or else a few minutes later. Care should

Two Smooth and one Wire puppies

be taken to count the afterbirths to make sure they have all been expelled. This can be difficult as the bitch usually eats these, though with a large litter it may be necessary to take them away from her and destroy them.

Provided everything has gone well, the bitch will completely relax and suckle her puppies as soon as all have been delivered. She should be offered a drink of milk and taken outside to relieve herself. While she is out the newspapers in the box can be changed. It is advisable to have her checked by a veterinary surgeon to make sure that no puppies or afterbirths have been retained, for these can set up very serious infections.

Most Dachshund bitches have normal whelpings, though some can suffer uterine inertia and may require pituitrin injections to stimulate their contractions. If these fail then a Caesarian section has to be performed. Bitches make excellent recoveries from these operations and a subsequent litter may be born perfectly normally. The main whelping problems seem to occur with the standard Wire-hair, in many cases for no apparent reason. They are perhaps the toughest of the six varieties, but the number of Caesarians that have to be performed is quite high.

For the first three weeks of life the puppies will just eat and sleep. The bitch should be given four feeds a day, two milky and two meat with added vitamins. At first she will be reluctant to leave the litter for any length of time but must be made to go out and relieve herself regularly.

Depending on the size of the litter, weaning should begin at about three weeks with the puppies being introduced to a saucer of puppy milk food. Their heads will have to be gently pushed towards the milk and the instinct to lap will come naturally.

Once they are lapping reasonably well, raw meat finely minced or scraped can be offered. The bitch must be taken away for longer periods until, by the age of six weeks, the puppies should be feeding well for themselves and the bitch's milk supply should be drying up. Her food too should have been cut down by this stage. Some mothers are very maternal and reluctant to leave a litter even going so far as to regurgitate their food for their puppies.

At about three weeks the puppies should be wormed for roundworms. Even if the bitch was wormed before mating, the puppies can still be badly infested. Various commercial preparations are sold for this purpose but it is essential to follow the manufacturer's directions exactly. Your veterinary surgeon can also provide you with the right drugs.

Outdoor puppy pen with shelter and water

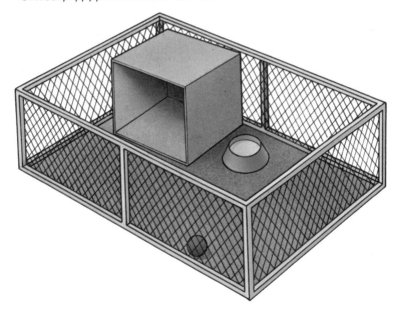

Throughout life a dog should be regularly wormed for roundworm but it is particularly necessary for puppies which can be killed by a bad infestation.

The puppies should be ready to go to their new homes by the age of eight weeks and the new owner should be given a diet sheet, pedigree and Kennel Club registration certificate.

Only if you have a really good dog should you consider using him at stud. The stud dog owner has a certain responsibility to the breed and should be prepared to refuse any bitch which he considers too bad a specimen to be bred. Unless your dog is a winning show dog, you will be unlikely to get any stud enquiries for him. A young winning dog should mate his first bitch at about twelve months of age and then be left until at least eighteen months before mating another. A pet dog who has never had the chance to mate a bitch in his youth is not likely to be a reliable proposition as a stud dog later on.

Health

Dachshunds as a rule are not prone to illness. They are a hardy breed provided they are kept in top condition. There is one complaint that they do tend to suffer from and of which prospective owners should be aware. Being long in the back, they are subject to slipped intervertebral discs. This can cause either complete paralysis in front or back legs or, in less severe cases, stiffness in the limbs associated with pain along the spine. When there is complete paralysis, there is great pain at first but this soon passes.

With modern veterinary techniques this condition can be cured quite successfully but it does need sympathetic and sometimes lengthy nursing. Heat in the form of an infra-red lamp is of beneficial value and so is massaging the affected limbs. Bladder and bowel control can be lost and the dog become incontinent. It is against both instinct and training for a dog to soil its bed and calm sympathetic nursing is particularly necessary to keep up the morale of such a patient. However, to see your Dachshund back on its feet after being paralysed is a marvellous sight and well worth the hard work it sometimes takes to achieve.

All puppies must be inoculated against hardpad, distemper and the two forms of leptospirosis and this is done between eight and twelve weeks of age. Boost inoculations should be given at the regular recommended intervals. Fortunately, through the wide use of vaccination these diseases are not so often encountered as they were.

Abscesses These can form anywhere on the body and are in the form of a swelling containing pus and blood. Bathing and a warm poultice will help to relieve the pressure and encourage the abscess to burst. The pus can then be gently squeezed out. It may take a few days for the abscess to drain, so the wound should be kept open by bathing. A large abscess will probably need antibiotic treatment.

Anal Glands These are enclosed in two pear-shaped sacs situated under the skin at each side of the anus. They are scent glands and produce a very foul smelling secretion which is normally discharged through a tiny pore at each side of the rectum. Sometimes these glands fail to empty and need

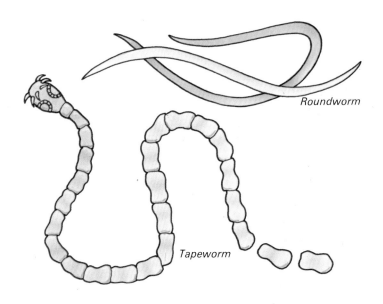

Roundworm

Tapeworm

Adult flea

Biting louse

Engorged female tick

Mite (microscopic)

Sucking louse

Parasites

expressing either by the vet or the owner. They can also become infected and need antibiotic treatment. A dog with anal gland trouble will often bite the area of its tail or slide along the ground on its bottom, both symptoms that can also mean a worm infestation.

Ears Otitis or canker can be caused by wax forming in the ear canal or by ear mites which can be picked up from cats. During the summer months grass seeds can cause much pain if they get in the ear. A dog with ear trouble will shake its head and repeatedly scratch its ears which will smell badly. Professional diagnosis and prescribed ear drops are really necessary.

Enteritis This is an inflammation of the bowel which can be caused by infection or by something the dog has eaten or occasionally by an allergy. The symptoms are diarrhoea and, in extreme forms, sickness as well. If it is caused by something the dog has eaten, the animal will not usually appear off-colour and a day's fasting will put matters right. However, if the dog appears lethargic or is passing blood, then veterinary assistance is needed as dogs can very easily become dehydrated and if left untreated this condition can be fatal.

Eclampsia This is a very serious condition in nursing bitches

Long-haired puppies

and needs urgent treatment. It is caused by lack of calcium and the bitch may appear drowsy or unsteady on her legs. There is often twitching of the muscles followed by convulsions. Treatment consists of injections of calcium. The bitch may have to be taken away from her puppies which will then have to be hand-reared.

Mastitis This can be caused by infection in the mammary glands of a nursing bitch. If there is only a small litter, it can also be caused by excess milk not being drawn off from all the teats. A hard, red and swollen teat which produces no milk when squeezed needs immediate attention as an abscess can form and the bitch become very ill. Antibiotic injections can be given and the area should be bathed frequently with a hot saline solution. By checking the teats every day, mastitis can be detected in its early stages when treatment is much easier.

Metritis The symptoms of this include an abnormal discharge from the uterus after whelping. It can be caused by the retention of a dead puppy or afterbirth, or by an infection. Veterinary treatment must be given.

Pyometra This is a condition where pus is formed in the uterus and is most common in middle-aged bitches. The bitch looks

Wire-haired miniature Dachshund

Long-haired miniature Dachshund

and feels very unwell with marked thirst, listlessness and vomiting. There is often a foul smelling discharge. Immediate veterinary action is required as this complaint can be fatal.

False Pregnancy Many bitches suffer from this to some degree or another. Although they have not been mated, they will show signs of being in whelp even going to the lengths of making a nest and producing milk. The psychological symptoms can cause the bitch a lot of distress and she should be encouraged to go out for walks rather than being left to brood in her bed. Tablets can be obtained to dry up the milk, or a pinch of Epsom salts given three times a day helps. Dachshunds do tend to have false pregnancies and they can cause the mammary glands to become rather baggy which can be a problem in a show animal.

Sore Pads These can be caused in a number of ways. Grass seeds can get in between the toes and, if undetected, can travel up the leg. A swelling will be noticed and this should be bathed with hot water and gently squeezed until the offending object is removed.

Cysts between the toes can be caused by grit or dirt getting in between the pads. Care of the feet can help to prevent this trouble, especially by keeping the feet of the Long-hair regularly trimmed. Treatment is by bathing the foot and waiting for the cyst to burst.

Cracked pads can be caused by either cutting the pad on glass, etc. or a reaction to certain substances on the roads or even in the home. These take some time to get better and, providing the wound is clean, can be left to heal naturally. Road walking should be suspended until the pad is healed.

Worms The two main types of parasitic worm to infect the dog are the roundworm and the tapeworm. All puppies are born with roundworms and should be treated as early as three weeks of age, and the treatment of all adults should be done on a regular basis. Tapeworms are usually only found in the adult dog when segments of the worm may be seen in the faeces or round the anus. Tapeworms are never passed directly from dog to dog but through an intermediate host, usually fleas or lice. Therefore when treating for tapeworms, the intermediate host must be treated as well.

Dogs can also suffer from whipworms, hookworms and heartworms. These are not common in Britain but are a problem in some states of America. Symptoms may include coughing, emaciation and general debility. Accurate diagnosis and treatment can be given only by a veterinary surgeon.

Any alteration of the dog's usual behaviour should be investigated in case it is the symptom of some health problem. Serious illness is indicated by an abnormally high or low temperature, persistent vomiting and diarrhoea, listlessness and loss of appetite or blood in the urine or faeces. One of the best indications of how urgent the problem is, will be the dog's temperature. This is taken in the rectum and is normally 101.5°F (38.6°C), though excitement or violent exercise will make it rise temporarily.

Taking a temperature is not difficult and is something that every owner should be able to do. Use a stubby ended thermometer and coat the bulb end with Vaseline. Stand the dog on a table and, if possible, get someone to hold the dog's head and place an arm under its stomach so that the animal cannot sit down suddenly. Insert the bulb end of the thermometer about 1in. (2.5cm.) into the rectum with a gentle twisting movement. Hold it in place for the length of time required, which is usually indicated on the thermometer itself. Any reading more than a degree above or below normal indicates that something could be seriously wrong. Remember to disinfect and shake down the thermometer after use.

READING LIST

Adler. *Dachshund.* T.F.H. Publications, 1966.

Brunotte, Hans. *Dachshund Guide.* The Pet Library Inc., 1969.

Fitch Daglish, E. *The Dachshund.* Popular Dogs Publishing Co. Ltd., 1968.

Harmar, Hilary. *Dogs and How to Breed Them.* John Gifford Ltd., 1974.

Lyon, McDowell. *The Dog in Action.* Howell Book House, 1966.

Portman Graham, Capt. R. *The Mating and Whelping of Dogs.* Popular Dogs Publishing Co. Ltd.

Raine, Katharine. *All About the Dachshund.* Pelham Books Ltd., 1972.

USEFUL ADDRESSES

The Kennel Club, 1 Clarges Street, Piccadilly, London W1Y 8AB, England.

The American Kennel Club, 51 Madison Avenue, New York, N.Y. 10010, U.S.A.

There are many clubs catering for this breed and the addresses of these can be obtained from your Kennel Club.

DOG MAGAZINES

Pure Bred Dogs, the American Kennel Gazette, published by the American Kennel Club.

Dog World, 22 New Street, Ashford, Kent, England.

Our Dogs, 5 Oxford Road Station Approach, Manchester 1, England.

Index

Distributors for
Bartholomew Pet Books

Australia

Book Trade: Tudor Distributors Pty. Limited, 14 Mars Road,
Lane Cove 2066, New South Wales, Australia

Canada

Pet Trade: Burgham Sales Ltd., 558 McNicoll Avenue,
Willowdale (Toronto), Ontario, Canada M2H 2E1
Book Trade: Clarke Irwin and Company, Limited,
791 St. Clair Avenue W., Toronto, Canada M6C 1B8

New Zealand

Pet Trade: Masterpet Products Limited,
7 Kaiwharawhara Road, Wellington, New Zealand
Book Trade: Whitcoulls Limited, Trade Department, Private Bag,
Auckland, Wellington, or Christchurch, New
Zealand

South Africa

Book Trade: McGraw-Hill Book Company (S.A.) (Pty.) Limited,
P.O. Box 23423, Joubert Park, Johannesburg,
South Africa

U.S.A.

Pet Trade: Pet Supply Imports Inc., P.O. Box 497, Chicago,
Illinois, U.S.A.
Book Trade: The Two Continents Publishing Group Limited,
30 East 42nd Street, New York, N.Y. 10017, U.S.A.